Wicca Spells

A Beginner's Guide to Wiccan Spells

Sarah Rhodes

Table of Contents

Introduction

Welcome, Wiccan!

Whether you are brand new to the craft, you've been practicing for a while, or you are just a curious bystander, we are so glad you could join us. This is the second installment in our *Wicca* series, and this time we'll be focusing on Wiccan spells. From the best time to cast a spell, to the different elements needed for the act of spellcasting, to writing your own spells, this book is your new go-to for all things magickal.

This book is all about spells, but before you go experimenting with magick, it's important to be aware of what it is you are practicing. We'll start off with some basics of the Wiccan religion; the history, what exactly Wiccans believe, how they practice, and so on. If you are a total newbie to the Wiccan fate, you might want to check out our first book *Wicca: A Beginner's Guide to Wiccan Magick*, where we take a deep dive into the history of the religion and all things regarding modern Wicca. If you already know all of that, feel free to skip the first chapter of this book. We won't judge you. If you're somewhere in the middle, allow us to offer up a quick refresher with Chapter 1.

The following chapters (2, 3, and 4) will cover some of the key elements that go into the act of casting a Wiccan spell. Namely these are the tools, the timeline, and the location. These chapters will help you to make sure you have all that you need—physically and mentally—to cast a spell.

Chapter 5 is what we're calling a Wiccan cheat sheet; here you'll find lists upon lists of materials, symbols, phrases, numbers, shapes, etc., as well as their corresponding properties and energies. Everything you need to be able to put your own spells together. And finally, we'll round off with a selection of spells that you can use in your own practice—or just refer to when you need some inspiration. These spells will cover love, luck, health, the home, and protection.

A Note on Witches

Before we get into the history of the religion, let us just clarify something: Not all witches are Wiccans, and not all Wiccans are witches.

Witches existed before Wicca was established, and a person can be a witch without subscribing to Wiccan ideals. There are also other Pagan religions that do not deal with witchcraft or magick of any kind. People sometimes use the words 'Wicca,' 'witch,' and 'Pagan' interchangeably, but they are not the same thing. The word 'Wiccan' was in fact only coined in 1954. So, it is important to note that any study or mention of witchcraft before the middle of the 20th century is not directly related to Wicca. The two are of course linked, but they are not the same.

There is just one rule that we like to push when it comes to Wicca: Do what feels best. If you don't like the word witch, don't use it. If you don't like the idea of calling yourself religious, don't do that. Wicca is a tapestry of beliefs and practices that you can tailor based on what feels best for you. If something isn't for you, that's okay. For the purposes of this book, a Wiccan is someone who practices the ritual of magick and subscribes to the key beliefs and philosophies of Wicca, and a witch is someone who only practices magick and/or witchcraft.

Whichever witch you wish to be, walk your path with the right intentions and you will be fine. Now, on to the magick!

Chapter 1: What is Wicca?

The Wiccan religion is simultaneously one that is laden with history, and one born of the New World. The word 'Wicca' was only coined in the 1950s, which is around the same time that the religion was formalized and established. However, the religion's beliefs and practices are all rooted in ancient history, predating Christianity and plenty of other organized religions by many, *many* years. Wicca is not an ancient religion, but it does give power and prominence to several ancient beliefs. That might sound slightly contradictory, so let's take a quick look at how exactly Wicca came around.

A Brief History

The base components of Wicca—such as the principal morals and beliefs, and the process of magickal rituals—stem from Pagan religions and practices that go back thousands of years, well before Christianity was established as a religion. This was so many years ago that it would be impossible to pin down the exact year that these Pagan rituals and beliefs began to form, so we won't even attempt to do that. Just know that these rituals and beliefs mainly consist of two core tenets: polytheism and the power of the natural world. More on this soon, but first let's look at how Wicca actually became a thing.

Many people attribute the organization of Wicca to a man called Gerald Gardner; while this is correct, the person who should probably be fully credited for the new modern interest in witchcraft is Dr. Margaret Murray. Murray was an Anglo-Indian anthropologist, Egyptologist, archeologist, folklorist, and historian who wrote *The Witch-Cult in Western Europe* in the year 1921. This was a study based on reports of the witchcraft trials and, when she published it, it was the first time that a scholar of note was looking at the subject of witchcraft with an unbiased eye. Up until this point, most work written on the subject seemed to stand by the early Christian belief that witchcraft in any form was the devil's work. *The Witch-Cult in Western Europe* presented the idea that witchcraft wasn't actually a form of Christian heresy, but rather, the practice of an old Pagan fertility cult that predated Christianity and survived the anti-Pagan purge of the Middle Ages.

As we mentioned in the Introduction, 'Wiccan' and 'witch' are not mutually exclusive titles, but the spread of witchcraft and magick in the New World contributed to what would eventually become Wicca. As the New World expanded, witchcraft turned into a mixture of many different beliefs and practices. Different cultures and customs existed side by side, often overlapping and creating new cultures and customs. So, while the Christians attempted to squash the religion in the Middle Ages (all the way until around 1750), the traditions and practices—rooted in folk magic—lived on. They simply moved underground.

These traditions would be passed down from family members, and these practicing witches would be referred to as 'fam trad witches.' Fam trad witches continued to practice their craft into the 18th and 19th centuries and would be the basis for research and studies such as those conducted by Dr. Murray.

It was Murray's research that would then give way to Gerald Gardner's active interest in witchcraft. This was during the mid-1940s, and many people still thought of witches as being evil, devil-worshiping women. Although Dr. Margaret Murray's work had gained a decent amount of attention, she wasn't exactly the number one best-selling author at the time. Gardner wanted more people to know that witches aren't evil women or con artists, but actually a group of people with a deep respect for nature, tradition, and folklore. He was a practicing witch and part of an underground coven at this time, but he felt that they shouldn't be forced to practice 'in secret.' However, at this time the Witchcraft Act of 1735 was still in place. This was a British parliamentary bill that claimed that it was still a crime for someone to claim that they had magical powers, and those convicted would be sentenced to a maximum penalty of one year in jail.

Because of this, Gardener couldn't exactly just announce himself and the rest of his coven to the world without risking jail time. His way around this was to write a historical novel called *High Magic's Aid* (published in 1949) that essentially explained everything that modern witches were up to but was framed as a fictional story. This was Gardner's first tiptoed step into the pool of magickal writing that would eventually lead to the organization of what we now call Wicca.

Gardner would lead his coven—and many other people interested in witchcraft—in the religion of Wicca. As Wicca gained popularity with younger people in Britain, it also traveled across the pond. Raymond Buckland is credited with taking Gardnerian Wicca over to the United States, along with his wife Rosemary. Buckland is an author and Wiccan who has written extensively on the topics of Wicca and witchcraft. In fact, if you are looking for a very detailed account on the history of witchcraft and how it evolved into Wicca, his book *Witchcraft From the Inside* is an essential read for practicing Wiccans. The Bucklands were originally from England, and they would become Gardner's first initiates to practice outside of the UK when they moved to the States in 1962.

By this time, Wicca had taken on a life of its own, independent of Gerald Gardner and his coven. The second-wave feminists of the late '60s/early '70s also had a lasting impact on the religion, making way for an increased focus on worshipping the Goddess and the divine feminine. Post-medieval religion—particularly Christianity—was very patriarchal, so any acknowledgement of a female deity was welcomed and encouraged. The '70s also saw a rise in what is called 'Eclectic Wicca,' which saw Wiccans combine a mixture of rituals and beliefs from different practices to suit their own journey, much like what Gardner himself had done 20 years prior. In fact, Gardnerian Wicca was falling slightly out of favor at this time, and different paths were slowly starting to form (we will discuss these shortly).

As witchcraft and Wicca grew in both popularity and visibility, they also attracted some unwanted attention. Some authors and directors included witchcraft in their work, often without doing the adequate research. A good example of this is the book-turned-movie *Rosemary's Baby*, published first in 1967 and adapted for the silver screen in '68. In the story, Ira Levin included characters that identified as witches, however the rituals they practiced were more akin to Satanic worship than actual witchcraft.

These characters weren't actually witches, but Ira Levin called them witches and consequently hundreds if not thousands of people decided they would start 'covens' and become 'witches' just like in the book/movie. But the fictional work did not accurately portray witchcraft, and this led to increased bad press for witches and Wiccans alike. This resulted in two things: the first is that some more unsavory characters began to identify as witches and Wiccans without actually subscribing to Wiccan beliefs, and the second is that Wiccans who were genuinely following the craft were again seen as evil-doers and devil-worshippers.

Despite this, the Wiccan religion continued—and still continues—to grow. By the end of the 20th century, several Wiccan churches and covens had been legally recognized as religious non-profit organizations, Wiccan priests and priestesses were present at institutions such as prisons, and more individuals would find enlightenment on their own path. The distinction between witches and Wiccans continues to remain somewhat murky, but to reiterate: not all witches are Wiccans, and not all Wiccans are witches. Some people will practice witchcraft and subscribe to the religion of Wicca, and some Wiccans will follow the religious beliefs but not practice the rituals or spellwork.

The rest of this book will focus on both the religious and magickal aspects of Wicca, and as the reader you are welcome to take them both on board, or just one, or neither. It's all up to you and what you feel is right.

Types of Wicca

The first type of Wicca to be recognized was Gardnerian Wicca, but compared to other paths there is not much to cover. Just know that it was the first organized form of Wicca. It focuses mainly on the divine power of nature, and often offers a basis for various other types of Wicca that have come into being.

Alexandrian

Perhaps the first variation on Wicca to set up after Gardnerian Wicca was Alexandrian Wicca. It was started in the UK in the 1960s by Alex and Maxine Sanders and is very much the same as Gardnerian Wicca save for two key differences. The first is a focus on gender polarity, i.e., recognizing a distinct difference between male and female energies in deities and in practitioners. The second is that Alexandrian is considered to be less strict than Gardnerian Wicca in its beliefs and rituals. The Alexandrian approach to religion and witchcraft is basically 'if it works, use it.'

Seax

This is a Wiccan path that is inspired by Anglo-Saxon pagan practices, beliefs, and iconography. Seax Wicca was founded in the USA in the '70s by Raymond Buckland and was the first type of Wicca to be practiced in America. Buckland's book *The Tree: Complete Book of Saxon Witchcraft* is considered to be the scripture followed by all Seax Wiccans. They also acknowledge and praise the Triple Goddess and the Horned God but refer to them as Freya and Woden, respectively. Seax Wicca is a traditionally coven-based practice, with High Priests and Priestesses elected democratically by vote on a yearly basis. It can, however, be practiced solitarily too.

Dianic

Dianic Wicca is a feminist branch of Wicca that is, for the most part, reserved for female Wiccans. It is essentially the same as Gardnerian and Alexandrian Wicca but gives focus to the Goddess and the earth's female energy. The main deity that followers praise is the Roman goddess Diana the Hunter, and they often practice meditation and visualization as a Coven alongside their spellwork. Traditionally, only women practice Dianic Wicca, but there is an offshoot of this path known as McFarland Dianic Wicca that accepts practitioners of either gender.

Celtic/Faery

Celtic Wicca takes the base principles of all Wicca and incorporates—as the name suggests—elements of Celtic mythology, such as the deities and seasonal festivals. Celtic Wicca teaches an intense love and respect for the earth and focuses on the magickal properties of plants, stones, herbs, trees, and so on. Celtic Wicca also acknowledges the existence of 'fae,' which are magickal creatures such as fairies, gnomes, and sprites.

Faery Wicca is an offshoot of Celtic Wicca that focuses solely on the existence of fae in place of any other deities. Both of these types of Wicca can be practiced solitarily, and you can self-initiate into the practice.

Odyssean

Inspired by the epic Greek poem *The Odyssey* by Homer, this path emphasizes the notion of one's life being a spiritual journey. Odyssean Wicca is one of the only Wiccan religions to provide public ministry, meaning that anyone who wishes to can attend services, rituals, and training, even if they are not initiated into the craft. However, it does not recognize the idea that people can practice on their own. It has a very intense focus on training, initiation, and degrees. You can attend a service or ritual if you are interested, but you cannot practice without the proper training and initiation.

Another interesting aspect of the practice is that Odyssean Wicca is a multi-pantheon-devotional polytheism practice. Those are a lot of words. What they mean is that followers believe that all the Gods and Goddesses from all ancient pantheons and belief systems are real and exist as separate entities.

Shaman

A person can identify as a Shaman without practicing Wicca, but in recent years the two practices have often crossed paths and intertwined to develop the combination of 'Shaman Wicca.' The main area of focus in this path is a deep connection with the spiritual realm and sacred beings. Many Shamanic Wiccans practice extensive meditation and projection in an attempt to reach a higher plane of consciousness and transcend the material realm. This is often done to seek answers to difficult questions and look towards the future.

Eclectic

The word 'eclectic' means something that draws on inspiration from various sources, and that is exactly what Eclectic Wicca is. This is currently the most popular Wiccan path, and those that practice it will pick and choose the beliefs, rituals, and deities that they most identify with. Some Eclectic Wiccans will come together to form an eclectic coven, but it is definitely a practice that is most popular amongst solitary Wiccans.

Other Paths

Some other Wiccan paths that we haven't discussed here include Green Wicca, Afro-Wicca, Draconic Wicca, Georgian Wicca, and Church-based Wicca, to name just a few.

Additionally, there are loads of new paths being developed constantly, as more and more people begin their journey into Wicca and forge new paths with fellow Wiccans. It is important to remember that there is no 'right' or 'wrong' way to practice Wicca. The 'right' way is the way that makes you feel comfortable.

Key Beliefs

As we've seen, Wicca comes in many different shapes and forms, and each individual Wiccan can practice in their own way. But as with any other religion, there are some basic beliefs that inform the way Wiccans practice their faith on a daily basis. The two key beliefs that are present in most practices are a belief in the deity (often in the form of the Triple Goddess and God) and acknowledgement of the divine power found within the natural world. We will cover these two beliefs here, as they work in tandem, as well as the Threefold Law. Some other popular

Wiccan beliefs include animism, reincarnation, divination, and astrology.

The Deities

There is no 'one true God' in Wicca. Rather, particular covens and solitary Wiccans will choose a deity from the vast number of pantheons and beliefs observed across the globe. There is no right or wrong choice when it comes to acknowledging a deity; rather, it depends on who you feel particularly drawn to on a personal level. Gods and goddesses from different pantheons often represent the same things but are depicted differently from culture to culture. The common thread in Wicca that runs through all beliefs and deities is that the divine power is present throughout all of the natural world. This belief originated in Gardnerian Wicca, which technically acknowledges just one Goddess and one God: the Moon and the Sun. Many Wiccans adopt these deities into their practice even if they do not fully align with Gardnerian thought, as it provides a clear line of connection between the divine and the earthly realms.

With the Sun God and the Moon Goddess, there is a balance of male and female energies present. The Goddess and the God go by many different names. You may hear them being referred to as the Lord and the Lady, the Deities, the Sun God and the Triple Goddess, to name just a few. In essence, Wiccans believe in a dual deity that is one-half goddess and one-half god. It is important to note that believing in a deity does not necessarily mean believing that there is an ancient man in the sky controlling us and judging everything we do. Joseph Campbell explains this concept of deity very clearly as "a reference to something that transcends all things," representing "the ultimate mystery of being" and existing "beyond all categories of thought." Placing this "mystery of being" onto a deity—in this case, the Goddess and the God—simply gives us somewhere to direct our beliefs and our energy.

Being a dual deity, the Goddess and the God are two halves of a whole. They exist separately but work in harmony with each other. One cannot exist without the other, just like yin and yang, or day and night. Wiccans believe that the deity is the original feminine and masculine force that makes all of life possible and is therefore present in all people and all things.

The Goddess is connected to the power of the moon, and—just as the moon has three key phases—the Goddess has three faces: The Maiden, The Mother, and The Crone. The God, then, is connected to the power of the sun and also has three faces: The Green Man, The Horned God, and The Sage. As the year goes by, the Goddess and the God undergo transformations and guide us—and each other—through our own personal transformations.

The Power of Nature

A belief in the power and divinity of nature is at the root of all Pagan beliefs, and therefore also the root of Wicca. Even before the Pagans, early civilizations connected the ideas of the divine with their surroundings. The elements, food, the skies, and so on were seen as things to be honored and worshiped. The divine was the force behind inexplicable progress and phenomena that ruled the natural world. Natural ingredients have also always been used in healing, medicine, and for nourishment.

As explained earlier, Wicca states that the Goddess and the God were the original forces that created life and are therefore present in all things. That means that all things, big and small, are physical manifestations of the deity and are in turn sacred and should be treated as such.

In addition to this belief is the knowledge that, before the Industrial Revolution and the age of Enlightenment came about and changed the way so many people lived, our ancestors only had nature to guide them through their daily lives. From navigation and shelter to food and medicine, through to light and heat, ancient civilizations had to harness the power of the earth to survive. Simply put, humans and nature worked in tandem to keep each other happy and healthy. And although in contemporary life technology has made our reliance on nature much less urgent, Wiccans still believe in working in tandem with nature to not only survive, but to thrive.

If the deity is present in nature, then nature has the divine power to guide us through our lives. And this power should not only be respected and cared for, but utilized and further energized through our Wiccan practices.

This divine energy that is spread throughout the earth can be divided into four main elements: fire, earth, air, and water. Wiccans harvest these elements in order to give power to their rituals and to inform their practice. Wiccans also acknowledge the existence of a fifth element: the element of the spirit. These elements work together to create life around us. Just like the Goddess and the God, the elements exist separately but work together. Again, one cannot exist without the other. If just one element were to disappear, the world as we know it would no longer exist. The elements each possess their own unique energy that can be harvested and brought into a Wiccan's magic.

Threefold Law

In Wicca, there is no one to tell you what you can and cannot do. If you will harm someone, there won't be anyone to come and stop you. However, Wiccans believe in the Threefold Law— sometimes also called the Law of Three.

This law states that whatever you put out into the world will come back to you three times. So, if you do something good, good will come back to you. And the same goes for negative intentions and energy. The 'three times' rule doesn't necessarily mean that three good things or three bad things will happen. But rather, it means that the energy that comes back to you will be three times that what you put out into the universe.

Wicca is all about you and your choices. Your choices will ultimately impact the rhythm of your life. So, if it doesn't harm anyone, follow your will. If it harms someone, be ready for your will to take you somewhere unpleasant. More on this when we discuss the Wiccan Rede in Chapter 4.

Chapter 2: Things You'll Need

There are three main elements to a Wiccan spell: intention, wording, and materials. The materials can come in the form of tools, ingredients, and symbols, which we will be covering in this chapter.

Tools and Ingredients

The below materials are all traditional and useful in Wiccan magick, but they are not all necessary. Each item has its own use, and you can choose the right things to add to your altar—which we will discuss in the next chapter—based on what kind of rituals you are performing.

Getting your hands on some of these tools and ingredients is as simple as buying a new cup or picking a flower from your backyard.

Athame

An athame is a sword or ritual knife, but it is never used to actually cut anything. Your athame is used for directing energy in rituals such as casting a circle, or to cut metaphorically through a bond. It generally has a black handle and an inscription on the blade (which can be blunt). It can be made of wood, stone, crystal, or metal, and you can decorate it as you wish.

It is useful to keep a separate knife at your altar to use for the cutting of herbs and rope, so that you do not accidentally use your athame for this.

Wand

If you are not comfortable using an athame in your ceremonies, a wand serves the same purpose. Typically made of wood or stone, with a tapered cylindrical shape that is wider at the end that you hold, it can also be decorated and inscribed. Choosing between a wand and an athame is generally a matter of personal preference; however, if you choose to work with fae in your craft, a wand is suggested. Fae are typically scared away by the presence of a knife or sword.

Chalice

A chalice is a cup that is used specifically at your altar and only for Wiccan ceremonies. It can be an ornate, expensive goblet or a simple mug. The important thing is that it hasn't been used for anything other than Wiccan ceremonies. The contents of the chalice—most often wine or water—are usually used as symbolic offerings for the deities.

Cauldron

A pot that is used to hold and burn items such as water, oils, papers, and herbs. It is generally made of cast iron and stands on three legs so that a source of heat can be placed underneath. However, any sort of pot or container can be used as long as it is able to withstand heat.

It is very important that your cauldron is thoroughly cleaned after ceremonies, spells, and rituals so as to avoid contaminating your next ritual.

Broom

No, brooms aren't used as a flying mode of transportation.

A broom is used to sweep away negative and unwanted energy from a space before casting a circle. You can make your own broom from wood, twigs, and rope, or you can buy one. If you buy one, be sure to select one that is made of only organic materials, as synthetic materials such as glue and plastic can inhibit the flow of energy.

Candles

Candles are used for a wide variety of things in Wiccan practice. They can be used to represent the element of fire, to represent a specific color's energy, or simply as a source of heat.

Many Wiccans will opt to have two specific candles to represent male and female energies. These candles are placed on the left and right of the altar respectively, and are generally a dark color such as blue, gray, or red for the male energy, and a lighter color such as gold, white, or rose for the female.

Divination Tools

If you practice divination, it is useful to keep your tools at your altar. These tools can include tarot cards, teacups and leaves, runes, a crystal ball, or a scrying mirror. Divination is an aspect of Wicca that not all Wiccans practice but is growing in popularity.

Knots

Quite simply, these are strings made of materials such as rope, or a scarf tied into a knot. These knots are used to contain or release energy. You can use a knot to symbolically bind the hands of an enemy, to preserve energy, or to secure an intention. The energy/intention is secured inside the knot when it is tied and is then released once the knot is undone. For this reason, knots are particularly useful for 'portable' spells. You can set the intention in one location and then release it somewhere else.

Stones and Crystals

Humans have always been drawn to gemstones and crystals throughout history. They have been used for aesthetic purposes as well as ritual ones. They are, after all, natural items created by the earth and therefore contain its divine power. Before using a stone in spellwork, it is recommended that they are washed with clear water and a natural, mild soap so that any unwanted energies are removed. Different stones and crystals contain different properties that can be used to direct energy and intention in spellwork, and they can be combined to create new energies. Refer to Chapter 5 for a list of stones/crystals and their corresponding properties.

Plants and Herbs

Just like with stones and crystals, these are natural materials that can be used in spellwork. Plants and herbs have different properties and inherent energies that can affect the outcome of a spell. They can be used as ingredients for food-based spellwork, or in the form of incense and essential oils to infuse the air or other items with their properties. Again, see Chapter 5 for specific details on these properties.

Symbols

Some rituals and spells will benefit from the inclusion of symbols that will strengthen the intention. These can be literal symbols such as depictions of the end goal (photos, items, or drawings) or figurative symbols (numbers, shapes, or colors) that carry appropriate energies to support the spell.

Animals

Images and depictions of animals will imbue spellwork with characteristics that are specific to the animal; they will help the Wiccan to embody those characteristics too. These characteristics come from popular culture formed over many years (e.g., we all think of bravery when we see an image of a lion), or they can come from personal thoughts and connections (e.g., if you feel comfort when looking at a puppy or brave when looking at a horse).

Colors

The symbolism and power of different colors affect everyone in their daily lives, beyond the practice of Wicca. Color theory is used in marketing, interior design, cooking, psychology... The list is endless. In Wiccan spellwork, color symbolism comes in many forms too. Some people will make a connection between the body's chakras and their representative colors, others the colors associated with different zodiac signs. Most commonly, however, individuals will use personal connection and association to imbue their spells with specific energies. Pink for love, green for money, red for passion, and so on. You can find a list of some colors and properties in Chapter 5; as with most things in Wicca, though, you can form your ritual based on personal preference and inclination.

Colors can be added into your spells in a variety of ways. Specific stones, crystals, and plants that contain natural pigmentation, colored candles, lights, food and drink, the clothes you are wearing... Color is all around us. In combination with your intention, the presence of the right colors will create the right energy for the spell.

Numbers and Shapes

Numerology is the belief that all numbers have a spiritual/magickal energy. Every person has a specific number based on their date of birth and the letters in their name, and this number will then affect their energy. Some Wiccans will choose to change their name, picking a new one based on the magickal properties related to numbers. The correspondence between letters and numbers is as follows:

- 1 = A, J, S
- 2 = B, K, T
- 3 = C, L, U
- 4 = D, M, V
- 5 = E, N, W
- 6 = F, O, X
- 7 = G, P, Y
- 8 = H, Q, Z
- 9 = I, R

Shapes are the way in which metaphysical patterns manifest themselves in the natural world, and (just like colors) they are found everywhere around us. Symbols like stars and crosses are present in many different religions, and often their meaning is understood differently across cultures. Shapes can be carved into candles, painted on surfaces, or made into talismans and pendants.

Chapter 3: The Wheel of the Year

The Pagan calendar did not go by days and months, because when it was created, days and months weren't a concept yet. Their calendar took the shape of a circle, or a wheel. The Wheel of the Year is divided into four quarters, one to mark each season. Wiccans follow the Wheel of the Year to inform their practice, and they celebrate key dates as religious holidays. The Wiccan calendar can be divided into two separate groups of holidays: Sabbats and Esbats. The Sabbats are marked on the Wheel of the Year, but the Esbats aren't. However, many Wiccans will refer to a Second Wheel in order to keep track of the full moons.

Throughout the four seasons, the Wheel tells a mythical story about the relationship between the Goddess and the God. The God, as the Sun, is born, grows strong, and ultimately dies in order to be reborn again. It also follows the agricultural cycles that were crucial for the survival of rural life and communities. The Esbats do the same to follow the journey of the moon (and the Goddess), as it journeys between crescent, full, and dark moon.

The sun and the moon are very prominent figures in Wicca. They are considered to be representative of the God and Goddess, but if you choose not to align your Wiccan practice with the existence of these deities, there is still benefit in observing the Sabbats and Esbats. On a purely physical level, the sun and the moon have an essential effect on the way our earth works and acknowledging the natural powers of the universe is at the heart of any Wiccan or Pagan religion.

The Sabbats

The Sabbats are Pagan holidays that all Wiccans celebrate. These holidays follow the change in seasons and the journey of the earth around the sun. They are dedicated to the masculine deity in the form of the Sun God. Since they are linked to the change in seasons, the dates on which these holidays are celebrated vary depending on whether you are in the northern or southern hemisphere. Some Sabbats are considered 'greater' or 'lesser' based on how high or low the Sun is in the sky because of the amount of energy it gives us. Below is a list of every Sabbat, the dates on which they are celebrated in both hemispheres, and a brief look at things you could do to celebrate the holiday.

Yule (Lesser Sabbat)

- Also known as the winter solstice
- 20–23 December (north)/June (south)
- This is when the sun reaches the southernmost point in the sky, and so it is the year's shortest day and longest night.
- Yule is a celebration of light amidst a time of darkness, as after this the days become longer and brighter.
- It is a time to prepare for renewal and new beginnings, and many Wiccans will use this time to plan for the year ahead.

- The festival of Yule is actually the Pagan precursor to the Christian holiday of Christmas, and many Yule celebrations are similar to Christmas ones. During Yule, you can use seasonal herbs, plants, and scents in your rituals and to decorate your altar. Some examples are pine, ivy, mistletoe, holly, cinnamon, cloves, and nutmeg.

Imbolc (Greater Sabbat)

- Also known as Brigid's Day or Candlemas
- 2 February/August
- On this day, we celebrate the earth beginning to warm up. It is not quite spring yet, but we are also no longer in the depths of winter.
- Imbolc is a time to clean and cleanse our spaces and our energies as we prepare for new life to populate the earth.
- This is a popular time for initiations: either self-initiation for solitary Wiccans, or into eclectic covens that don't necessarily have a specific day for initiation.
- Ingredients that you can use for rituals at this time include wild flowers, poppy seeds, sunflower seeds, and oats.

Ostara (Lesser Sabbat)

- Also referred to as the spring equinox
- 19–22 March/September
- At this point, day and night are perfectly balanced and equal in length, so it is a good time to practice balance in our lives too.
- Ostara is all about fertility and growth, as well as care and nurturing. This can mean in animals and nature, as well as in ourselves. It is a good time to check in on your progress and reflect on any practices that might not have been given enough attention.
- The goddess Ostara is often represented in the form of a hare, and this time is dedicated to celebrating the fertility of farm animals, so images of eggs, lambs, and rabbits are extremely popular (similar to during Easter).
- Some herbs, plants, and scents that will be beneficial to rituals at this time include lemon, lilies, strawberries, rose, and lavender.

Beltane (Greater Sabbat)

- Also known as May Day
- 31 April–1 May/October–November
- Beltane happens at the peak of spring and is all about fertility, sexuality, and passion.

- This is a particularly Pagan festival, and many non-Wiccan cultures will celebrate May Day by dancing around a maypole (which is considered to be a phallic symbol).
- Beltane celebrates fertility and sexuality in people and the love that brings them together, but it also celebrates the fertility of the earth and the gifts that it gives us. For this reason, you can use any seasonal flowers and leaves you can access in your rituals and at your altar.
- Other popular ingredients are vanilla, paprika, jasmine, and oats.

Litha (Lesser Sabbat)

- Also celebrated as Midsummer or the summer solstice
- 20-24 June/December
- As it marks the beginning of summer, Litha takes place on the longest day and shortest night of the year. On this day we celebrate the light being at its peak before we return to the dark in the coming months.
- Litha comes just before the harvest, so we prepare for this.
- Since the sun is at its peak this also means its energy is strongest at this time; this will aid any rituals that require lots of energy, such as dreamwork.

- Litha is a perfect time to work with fae, as they will also be out and about enjoying the sun!
- At your altar and in rituals you can use citrus, sage, paprika, and honey.

Lammas

- Also called Lughnasadh
- 1 August/February
- This is a celebration of the harvest and all the gifts that the earth has provided us with.
- Lammas is a great time to make your own broom with the leftover corn, reed, or wheat from the harvest.
- Bread and baking are a key part of celebrating and expressing thanks for the harvest.
- Try to use homegrown and local produce both in your daily meals, as well as in your rituals and spellwork.

Mabon

- Also celebrated as the autumn equinox
- 21-24 September/March
- During Mabon, the day and night are equally long once again; after this, we begin to lose the light. We use this time to offer thanks to summer and the sun

for the energy and produce that we have been provided with.

- This is a good time to tie up any loose ends as we approach winter and the end of the harvest season. Popular spells during Mabon will be cleansing and preparation spells in your house or personal space.
- At your altar and in rituals you should try to use the leaves, pines, and acorns that fall naturally from the trees during autumn.

Samhain

- Sometimes also referred to as Halloween
- 31 October - 1 November/April - May
- This is the final Sabbat on the Wheel of the Year and a time for celebration before the arrival of winter.
- During Samhain, the veil between the realms of the living and the dead is at its thinnest; this makes it a good time to practice spellwork that aims to contact the dead.
- It is a time to celebrate our loved ones who have passed and to recognize that there is no life without death, just as there is no light without dark.
- Samhain is also a good time to practice divination.
- Popular foods at this time are corn, apples, and pumpkin. In your rituals you can use rosemary, mint, cinnamon, and garlic.

The Esbats

The Esbats are celebrated roughly every 29/30 days, in conjunction with the full moon each month. There are 12 Esbats—one for every month. Just as the Sabbats praise the energy of the sun and the masculine deity, the Esbats do the same for the moon and the feminine. The names of these moons will vary based on the Wiccan path you follow, and they all have several names, so don't be surprised if you see them being referred to as something else in other sources. Really, knowing the name of the moon is not as important as knowing what it stands for and how to celebrate it.

January

- The Cold Moon
- Focus on promoting individuality and shaping your own unique Wiccan practice.
- Pay attention to communication and use your spellwork to encourage better communication with yourself, your deities, and the people you encounter on a daily basis.

February

- The Quickening Moon

- A time to look ahead and make plans
- February's moon will promote divination and reaching out to the spiritual side of life in search of signs.

March

- The Storm Moon
- Focus on your temperament during this moon, and practice patience in your rituals and spellwork.
- Use this time to reconcile any damaged bonds in your personal life, and maybe offer up an apology to someone you have wronged.

April

- The Wind Moon
- The energy of April's moon will aid you in the manifestation of your goals, so meditation and visualization will be very effective this month.
- It is also a good time to focus on courage and maybe any evidence of stubbornness that might be holding you back from reaching your goals.

May

- The Flower Moon
- Use your spellwork and rituals to focus on your potential and encourage growth, either in a particular skill or any elements of your personality that may be lacking maturity.
- May's moon will also give power to fertility.

June

- The Sun Moon
- Take a look at where change of any kind is needed in your life and direct your energy towards it.
- June is about transformation in any form: manifest or banish, increase or decrease.

July

- The Blessing Moon
- If you have had any plans sitting idly, July is a time to get them moving.
- Use your spellwork and rituals to promote productivity in the coming winter months.

August

- The Corn Moon
- A time to clean and cleanse, both your personal energy and your physical space.
- Prepare for a time of solitude and encourage a peaceful approach to the colder months.

September

- The Harvest Moon
- Focus on building strong foundations in your relationships with everyone in your life (including yourself).
- A time to promote love of all kinds.

October

- The Blood Moon
- Encourage balance and justice with your rituals and spellwork, and focus on elements of your life that seem to be thrown off-kilter.
- October's moon will give strength to divination practices and make communication with the spirit world easier.

November

- The Mourning Moon
- Release any emotion that has been holding you back from either reaching personal goals or otherwise being your best self.
- Banish any negative energy taking over your mind or your space.

December

- The Long Night Moon
- Prepare yourself for the coming year and focus on balancing your inner and outer lives.
- Be ready for external truths to be brought to light as others also prepare for the coming year.

Chapter 4: In Preparation for Spellcasting

The act of casting a spell takes both practice and preparation. Preparation comes mainly in the form of research and meditation, as well as the physical preparation of a space in which to practice.

Book of Shadows

A Book of Shadows is a hand-written book that is unique to a coven or solitary Wiccan. It contains religious texts, instructions for rituals, information on beliefs and values, and spells to be practiced. In a coven, there will be one collective Book of Shadows that all members will refer to. Members of a coven will sometimes write out their own copies for personal reference, but their own copy won't vary in any way from the one approved by the founders and/or High Priest or Priestess. A collective Book of Shadows that is passed down in covens and families is sometimes also called a Grimoire.

In Eclectic and solitary Wicca, a Book of Shadows is a lot more personal and sometimes serves as a journal as well as a sacred text. You can use your Book of Shadows to collect magickal lore that you come across, information on the properties of specific herbs and plants, spells you are learning or working on, and so much more. For Eclectic and solitary Wiccans, a Book of Shadows is considered something extremely personal, and there aren't many rules when it comes to making your own. A good way to start your Book would be to write down a protection spell and the Wiccan Rede—or any other moral code—on the first few pages. After that, you can fill out the rest of it with your own writing and research, as well as some drawings too. You also don't need to fill it out all at once; just like a journal, you can add more to your Book of Shadows as you learn and grow in your craft.

You should keep your Book of Shadows at your altar with your other Wiccan tools, mostly out of convenience. Your Book of Shadows can obviously be brought out and about with you— again, this is a personal object—but keeping it at your altar means you won't ever forget where it is!

The Wiccan Rede

The Wiccan Rede is a set of moral codes that Wiccans live by in both their religious practice and their daily life. It can be found in the form of a long poem, and Wiccans often write it down at the start of their Book of Shadows. The origins of the Rede are somewhat disputed. Some people believe that Gerald Gardner wrote it, but the first recorded version of it is attributed to Doreen Valiente—a member of Gardner's coven—in 1964. It is also believed that the full version—known as the Long Rede— was actually written in 1974 by a woman named Phyllis "Gwen" Thompson. The full version of this Long Rede is below, but the Wiccan Rede is generally considered to be just the final line of this poem: 'An ye harm none, do what ye will.'

> Bide the Wiccan Laws we must In Perfect Love and Perfect Trust.

> Live and let live. Fairly take and fairly give.

> Cast the Circle thrice about to keep the evil spirits out.

To bind the spell every time let the spell be spake in rhyme.

Soft of eye and light of touch, speak little, listen much.

Deosil go by the waxing moon, chanting out the Witches' Rune.

Widdershins go by the waning moon, chanting out the baneful rune.

When the Lady's moon is new, kiss the hand to her, times two.

When the moon rides at her peak, then your heart's desire seek.

Heed the North wind's mighty gale, lock the door and drop the sail.

When the wind comes from the South, love will kiss thee on the mouth.

When the wind blows from the West, departed souls will have no rest.

When the wind blows from the East, expect the new and set the feast.

Nine woods in the cauldron go, burn them fast and burn them slow.

Elder be the Lady's tree, burn it not or cursed you'll be.

When the Wheel begins to turn, let the Beltane fires burn.

When the Wheel has turned to Yule, light the log and the Horned One rules.

Heed ye flower, Bush and Tree, by the Lady, blessed be.

Where the rippling waters go, cast a stone and truth you'll know.

When ye have a true need, hearken not to others' greed.

With a fool no season spend, lest ye be counted as his friend.

Merry meet and merry part, bright the cheeks and warm the heart.

Mind the Threefold Law you should, three times bad and three times good.

When misfortune is enow, wear the blue star on thy brow.

True in love ever be, lest thy lover's false to thee.

Eight words the Wiccan Rede fulfill: An ye harm none, do what ye will.

Sacred Spaces

A sacred space can be fixed and permanent, such as one that is set up in your home or bedroom, or it can be portable and set up where and when needed. A space is essentially made up of two components: an altar and a circle.

Altars

Okay, so we've been telling you about things to keep at your altar, but what about the altar itself? At its most basic, an altar is a flat surface that is reserved for Wiccan objects and rituals. It can be anything from a large table to a small wall shelf, or even a marked-off area of your floor or shelf inside a cupboard. Some Wiccans will have a permanent altar set up, called a Devotional Altar, that is simply used for prayer and worship. Others will have a temporary altar, called a Ritual Altar, which is only set up when needed. Some will create an altar that is a mixture of the two. An altar is used for all forms of Wiccan magick and reflection, and (just like the Book of Shadows) it is a very personal aspect of your practice. You can set up and decorate your altar however you like, using any of the tools we just went over and other images and symbols that you consider relevant.

Once you've identified a surface to use, you can begin setting it up. Many Wiccans will opt to begin with a surface cover, such as a piece of cloth or material. The purpose of this cover is twofold: aesthetics and practicality. A cloth is easy to pick up and wash in the event of a spill or similar mishap during a spell (we've all been there, don't worry), and it can also add a pleasant element of color and design to the space. Sometimes this cloth might include colors and shapes that you feel will be beneficial to your practice or are relevant to the season. You could even paint directly onto the surface if you're feeling crafty.

The next step would be to identify what tools, statues, candles, and other items you want to keep at your altar. If you work with crystals, you could set them up permanently here, and you could keep a statue or devotional candle in honor of your preferred deity (or deities). Your chalice, cauldron, athame, etc. can be placed at the altar, or you could store them elsewhere and bring them out as and when needed. Again, we will say this for all things Wicca: it's up to you. Do what feels best and most beneficial to your own practice.

Circles

The next important space that needs to be established for rituals and spellworking is a circle. Unlike your altar, the circle is not a fixed, physical space. A circle is only set up—or cast—when magickal work is being done. A circle is a perimeter of energy—sometimes marked off physically, but not necessarily—that protects you as you practice your magick. It helps to focus your magickal energy towards the task at hand, and also acts as a barrier against unwanted energy.

A circle—like a church or temple—is a sacred space and should be treated as such. It is a space that establishes a connection between the material and spiritual world, existing outside of space and time. It is a space that is created through energy and visualization, but you may opt to mark it off physically for better focus. You can mark your circle off with things like salt, oats, chalk, stones, herbs, crystals, and candles, based on where and why you are casting your circle. The circle is drawn or marked off in the space you are practicing your magick and should be large enough to fit all those practicing inside of the circle. For many solitary Wiccans, this space will be in your home and in front of your altar. If your ritual does not include the invocation of any deities, a circle is not entirely necessary, but you may opt to draw one out for ease of focus and to establish a magickal boundary.

Regardless of if you draw or mark out an actual circle on the floor, it is important to mark out the four quarters of the circle.

These quarters represent the four cardinal directions and their respective elemental energies (listed in the next chapter). These quarters are often—but not always—represented by candles. The first step for many Wiccans in casting a circle will be to 'call the quarters.' This is done by journeying around the circle clockwise and lighting each candle, beginning from the east to follow the journey that the sun makes around the earth. If you are not working with candles, you could sprinkle saltwater around the perimeter of the circle or carry burning incense or a wand/athame in your hands as you travel around the circle. As you call the quarters, be sure to visualize the energy from the earth traveling up from the ground, through your body, and out through your fingers (or the tool that you are holding).

When you are done with your ritual, spell, or adoration, it is important to close off your circle before carrying on with your day. If you invoked any deities, thank them for their protection, and repeat your journey around the circle and the quarters—counterclockwise, this time. Extinguish any candles or collect crystals from the ground. If you used a wand, athame, or incense to visualize the perimeter, be sure to repeat this process—this time visualizing the energy returning to the ground. Take a moment to ground yourself too before exiting the space where the circle was and carrying on with your day.

Energy

The most important thing to know is that the energy you are using in magick and spellwork is not your own energy. You are simply borrowing it from the earth. Additionally, this energy is neutral: it is neither positive nor negative. Your will and the way you choose to direct this neutral energy will then affect the outcome of the spellwork.

Energy exists all around us and in all things: every animal, plant, and person. This energy is the divine energy that we have discussed earlier in this book and is given to the earth by the deities. Accessing this divine energy takes a certain amount of mental strength. Just like with physical strength, you need to exercise and train it. You also need to warm up to avoid mental strain, meaning you cannot just go straight into a ritual or spell.

Grounding

Before starting a ritual, many Wiccans will begin by practicing something called 'grounding.' There are two aspects to this: The first is to 'shake off' negative or unwanted energy, and the second would be to attune yourself with your surroundings to access the divine energy around you. How you choose to shake off your negative energy is entirely personal. You could actually physically shake it off, do some yoga or physical exercise, or engage in meditation or mindfulness exercises. Even the simple acts of taking a shower or eating a meal can help you to feel grounded. If you are feeling tired, or are lacking your own personal energy, grounding will help you to better access the earth's energy and direct it appropriately.

Shielding

Once you feel grounded, you need to direct your energy correctly. Otherwise, you could end up sending your energy all over the place. To direct this energy, you need to put some boundaries in place—also referred to as the act of shielding.

'Shielding' is basically creating a barrier around yourself while practicing ritual magick which gives you control over what energies impact your practice. This barrier can be metaphorical—established by engaging a mental shield against negative influences—or it can be physical. This is where the act of casting a circle comes in.

Visualization

Finally, visualization is a technique that Wiccans often use to support the direction and flow of their energy.

The idea is that you need to transform your thoughts from words into images, because images are generally more impactful and will give your energy more power. If you think of the visual aspect of something—as opposed to just thinking of its name—you will have a clearer idea of what you are aiming for. Thinking of what the sea looks like is more effective to your memory than just thinking of the word 'sea,' and similarly, visualizing your plant growing will be more effective for your growth spell.

In order to strengthen your visualization skills, all you really have to do is train yourself to think in images. Here is an example of an exercise you can carry out to help train your brain:

Hold up something in front of you, like a keychain or this book, and look at it closely. Feel it, too. Consider the colors, the textures, how it feels in your hands, what it smells like; take in all the details you possibly can. Now put it down, close your eyes, and try to remember those details. Try and recreate the item in your memory, from the shape and color to the weight and smell.

When the details fade from your mind's view, open your eyes, and look at it again. How closely did you recreate it?

Repeat this exercise with this object until you feel confident in your ability to visualize it, and then move on to a new one. If you are feeling especially confident, you can try to memorize and visualize several objects at once. And then you can do it with your entire room, a person, or an animal. With practice, you'll notice your ability to visualize improve quite a lot!

Chapter 5: Wiccan Cheat Sheets

Use this chapter as a quick reference for all things Wiccan and magickal.

Here you can find information on a whole bunch of things that you might use in a spell, from colors to herbs to key words and everything in between.

Well, we say everything, but if we really were to list everything this book would be 2000 pages long. There are loads of things that can be used in Wiccan magick. At the very least, there is an infinite amount of numerical combinations and a never-ending spectrum of colors.

This is a pretty comprehensive list of lists though, so let's say it's *almost* everything in between.

Elements

Air	intelligence, inspiration, optimism, east, spring
Water	compassion, insecurity, forgiveness, west, fall
Earth	foundation, nourishment, healing, north, winter
Fire	love, enthusiasm, destruction, passion, south, summer
Spirit	divine connection beyond the earth, the Wheel of the Year

Colors

Red	passion, love, sex, strength, danger, power, bravery
Orange	happiness, creativity, expression, ambition, success
Yellow	warmth, energy, friendship, pleasure, knowledge, growth
Green	abundance, healing, growth, nature, finances, fertility
Blue	peace, water, focus, clarity, luck, truth
Purple	wisdom, spirituality, breaking habits, mystery, meditation
Pink	love, friendship, society, care, peace, kindness
Gold	fortune, the sun, masculinity, attraction, wealth, power
Silver	intuition, the moon, femininity, dreams, meditation
Brown	comfort, home, gardens, stability, strength, healing
Black	wisdom, safety, defense, pride, power, grounding
White	purity, innocence, wishes, healing, balance, protection

Herbs/Plants

Basil	love, good luck, anti-anxiety
Caraway	loyalty, memory
Dandelion	purification
Elder (flowers and berries)	calming, liberation
Fennel	sexuality, fertility, strength
Ginseng	luck, desire, attention
Holly	protection from evil, prosperity
Juniper	protection from theft
Lavender	clarity of thought, peace
Mint	energy, comfort
Parsley	passion, fertility
Rosemary	memory, youth, cleansing
Sage	wisdom, awareness, cleansing
Thyme	renewal, purification
Vanilla	happiness, energy, love
Willow	identity, inspiration

Gems/Stones/Crystals

Amber	protection
Citrine	abundance
Diamond	commitment, trust
Emerald	divination, clarity
Garnet	health, creativity, bravery
Hematite	grounding, aura protection
Jade	prosperity, longevity
Lapis Lazuli	focus, thought, meditation
Moonstone	dreams, soothing of emotions
Onyx	absorbing negative energy, breaking bad habits
Pearl	self-esteem, happiness, confidence
Quartz (smoky)	protection, focus, survival
Ruby	passion, love, openness
Sapphire	connection, spiritual knowledge
Turquoise	health, anti-pollution, cleansing

Numbers

1	the force that connects all living things, a source of power, grounding
2	polarity and duality, balance, relationships with our surroundings
3	the most magical number, the triple goddess, action and interaction
4	the four elements, the cardinal directions, the seasons, compassion
5	the spirit, the human senses, points of a pentagram, chaos and conflict
6	the sun, masculinity, security, power, responsibility
7	the moon, femininity, intuition, wisdom, consciousness
8	the Sabbats, divine communication, longevity
9	power, change, growth, journeys, completion
0	potential, cleansing, beginnings

Shapes

Circle	unity, wholeness, life cycles, the full moon
Circle with line ⊖	refusal, banishing
Square ☐	foundations, stability, permanence, truth
Triangle, up △	male energy, fire
Triangle, down ▽	female energy, water
6-pointed star ✡	air, water, fire, earth, spirit
Star ☆	hope, wishes, dreams, protection
Cross ✝	creation, male/female, heaven/earth, spirit/matter
Arrow ↗	energy, aim, focus, precision
Spiral	reflection, a spiritual journey, life's energy

Months

Note: The below list follows the calendar according to the seasons in the Northern Hemisphere and simply lists the relevant Wiccan holidays. For more detailed information on each month and its celebration(s), refer back to Chapter 3.

January	The Cold Moon
February	Imbolc, The Quickening Moon
March	Ostara, Spring Equinox, The Storm Moon
April	Beltane, The Wind Moon
May	Beltane, The Flower Moon
June	Litha, Summer Solstice, The Sun Moon
July	The Blessing Moon
August	Lammas, The Corn Moon
September	Mabon, Autumn Equinox, The Harvest Moon
October	Samhain, The Blood Moon
November	Samhain, The Mourning Moon
December	Yule, Winter Solstice, The Long Night Moon

On Creating Your Own Spells

Writing your own spells, even if just as practice, is a good way to get attuned with your Wiccan practices and preferences.

A Wiccan spell can be of any length and in any language (of course, for the purposes of this book we will be looking at phrases in English). It can be written in verse or prose, recited out loud or internally, spoken or sang. Again, it is all about personal preference.

To write your own spell, there are four main elements you need to identify as your starting points:

- the purpose/intention of your spell (what you hope to gain)
- what tools/ingredients you need or want to use
- the right words to express your intention, and to invoke and thank the deities
- when you should cast your spell (the best day and time)

The tools, symbols, and ingredients you choose to include in a spell should work to support, strengthen, and balance each other, as well as to direct the appropriate energies and properties. More importantly, though, you should pick items that you are comfortable working with. Certain stones or herbs will serve the same purpose, so choosing which to work with is entirely a matter of personal preference, or simply availability. There isn't a right or wrong choice here, but if you work with a tool you are not entirely comfortable with, your energy might have an effect on the spell's outcome.

Writing your own spell isn't entirely necessary. Many books on Wicca—this one included, obviously—will provide you with ready-written spells that you can cast or use as templates and starting points.

If you do wish to write an original spell, the words you use need to address some specific areas. Make sure that you:

1. Invoke the deities or elements: If you align yourself with one specific god or goddess, you might ask for their protection. Alternatively, you could call in a specific deity related to the spell you are casting, or just ask for some spiritual or divine energy from the earth and the heavens.

2. State your intention: Let it be made clear what the reason behind your spell is, perhaps why you are casting it, or what the desired outcome is.

3. Cast the spell: This pertains to the physical actions taken to activate your tools and ingredients; it does not always need to be recited, but some Wiccans opt to narrate their actions and movements for the sake of focus and clarity.

4. Give thanks: Thank the spirits or deities for their protection during your spell and for the outcome of your spell.

Make sure that before you begin performing any ritual or spellwork you cast your circle, as explained in Chapter 4, and that you close it once you are done. Similarly, if you called on any deities at the start of your spell/ritual, make sure to thank them when you are done.

Some Phrases

When you read spells, you will often see some phrases repeated that have a particular 'prayerful' or ritualistic sound to them. The language you use in your spells can be simple and more reminiscent of everyday speech, but including an element of ritual in the words you choose can help you to direct your energy and get in the right headspace.

Here we'll explain some key phrases you can include in your spells:

1. I call on [name of deity]: If you are asking for the help or protection of a specific deity, you should call on them to

join you in your ritual. Verbally calling them into the space will use your vocal energy to focus your attention and that of the deities.

2. As above, so below: a reminder that everything that happens in the material realm is mirrored in the spiritual realm, and vice versa. Everything is a part of a pattern, and we play a part in that—especially when working with magick.

3. For the good of all, may it harm none: These words emphasize the Wiccan ideal to never will any harm onto others with our magick and they help to guide the energy towards the best possible outcome.

4. So mote it be: Many Wiccans will choose to end their spell with these four words to seal their intention.

5. Be gone: If the spell's intention is to banish a negative being or energy from a space or person, these words act as a 'period' or 'full stop' to the sentence.

We will now close off this book with a selection of spells that you can use yourself in your magickal practice. Not all of these spells include a spoken element, and they are by no means the only way to achieve each goal. Please feel free to alter them, change out the ingredients and tools, or add some text according to your personal preference. Just be sure to keep everything in the present tense and to be clear with your intention in order to avoid any misdirected energy or unwanted outcomes. And always keep the Threefold Law and Wiccan Rede in mind as you work.

Chapter 6: Spells for Love

To Make New Friends

Intention:

If you recently moved somewhere new or have fallen out with old friends, this spell is perfect for attracting new people to your social life.

You will need:

- Rose quartz, carnelian, or lapis lazuli
- A yellow candle
- Lavender essential oil
- Optional: a pink velvet/flannel bag

Steps:

Place the stone(s) you have chosen directly in front of your candle. Anoint your candle with some lavender oil, and then light it. Pick your stone(s) up and place them in the palm of your dominant hand, and then cover them with the other hand.

Visualize yourself surrounded by new friends (or just one new friend if that's what you're after) and direct the energy that you take from the ground into your hands. As you do that, recite the following:

Those around me kind and true,

Let us together establish friendships new.

So mote it be.

Place the stones back onto your altar and extinguish the candle. You may wish to put the stones into a small pink bag so that you can carry them with you when you go out.

Before a First Date

Intention:

If you're heading out on a first date—be it with a stranger or someone you already know who is looking to romance you—it's perfectly normal to feel a bit nervous. This spell will boost your confidence and lead you on to a great first date!

You will need:

- A basil leaf or a pearl (or both)
- A pink ribbon
- Sea salt
- Wand/athame
- A red candle

Steps:

Lay the ribbon flat on your altar and sprinkle the sea salt in a circle around it. Place the basil leaf/pearl on top of the ribbon, at the center of the circle. Light your candle. Pick up your wand or athame and pass it over the flame of your candle, then around the circle of sea salt and across the ribbon. As you do so, recite the following:

I am secure in my own skin

and it will be evident without and within.

As I head out to meet someone new

this for the two of us will be true.

So mote it be.

Wrap your leaf/pearl in the ribbon and secure it with a knot. Pick up some of the sea salt, sprinkle it on top of the secured ribbon, and extinguish your candle. As with the previous spell, you can place the ribbon inside a small cloth bag and keep it on you during the date. Just remember to throw it out if you were using a basil leaf!

To Attract a New Love

Intention:

If you are looking to bring some romance into your life and beat the single blues, or you have your eyes on a particular person, this spell will help to direct some of that romantic energy your way and bring a new love into your life.

You will need:

- Rose petals
- A red candle
- Rose, gardenia, or jasmine essential oil or incense
- Rose quartz
- Cauldron/fireproof dish
- A red cloth bag
- Pen and paper

- If you are thinking of someone in particular: a photo of them

Steps:

On a piece of paper, write out the attributes that you are looking for in a new love. These should be both physical preferences and character traits that you are attracted to. If you are aiming to attract the love of a specific individual, you can include a photo of them too.

In your cauldron or on your dish, place your rose petals. If you are using artificial petals, place them in a circle around the dish instead. Anoint your candle with your chosen essential oil, and then light it. If you are using incense, light this alongside your candle.

Run your paper (and photo if using one) through the flame of your candle until it ignites and place it inside your dish while it burns to ash. Once the fire has fully extinguished, place your rose quartz inside the dish with the ashes and petals. Allow the contents to cool.

When they are cool enough to be touched, empty the contents of your dish into your cloth bag and seal it. Extinguish your candle (and incense if used). Place the bag under your pillow or bed until your new love has found their way to you.

Chapter 7: Spells for Luck and Abundance

For Good Luck

This spell is relatively easy but can lead to exciting results. It is good for beginners who are looking to bring some good luck into their lives.

You will need:

- Orange or green candle
- Ginseng essential oil
- A stick of cinnamon
- Dish

Steps:

Anoint your candle with the ginseng oil and pass the cinnamon stick over the flame briefly. Place the cinnamon down onto your dish and recite the following:

With this cinnamon,

I bring good luck to me.

As I do good for others,

it returns by the power of three.

Extinguish your candle. You can leave the cinnamon stick on your altar for a while, or you could even use it in some baking and share with others to bring them some luck too. Apple and cinnamon muffins are always a good idea.

A Blank Check

This charm will lead you to abundant financial prosperity or will help you to make a specific amount of money. Whether you are saving for a specific purpose, or you just want to watch the cash rolling in, give this a try.

You will need:

- A blank check or a template
- Gold, silver, or dark-green pen/marker
- Gold, silver, or dark-green candle
- Patchouli or cinnamon essential oil
- A frame or clear plastic folder

Steps:

Anoint your candle with your essential oil of choice. Place your blank check on your altar and fill it out as follows. Address the check to yourself, writing down your full name. For the amount, write down 'unlimited.' Alternatively, you could just write down a specific amount that you are aiming to make. But why not just ask for it all? Write down the date by which you need the money, or choose a date that has some personal significance.

When you are done, pass the check over (not through!) the candle flame, and place it inside your frame or folder. Extinguish the candle. Display the check somewhere prominent in the space where you practice your magick.

Moon Money Charm

This is a simple spell that will protect your financial stability and help you to make informed financial decisions.

<u>You will need:</u>

- A collection of coins, ideally silver
- A ceramic bowl
- Sea salt (about 1 tsp)
- Water
- A basil leaf (chopped) or patchouli essential oil
- A dark-blue or dark-green cloth bag

<u>Steps:</u>

Fill the bowl with water and mix in the sea salt and basil/essential oil. Use your wand or athame to mix. Place the coins in the bowl, and then place the bowl by a window or outside to charge under the moon overnight. If you can, do this on the night of the full moon.

The following morning, take the coins out of the bowl, wipe them down, and place them inside your cloth bag. Keep the cloth bag next to something reminiscent of your finances, such as your wallet or documents related to banking.

Chapter 8: Spells for Health

To Promote Good Health

<u>Intention:</u>

This spell doesn't target a specific illness or injury, but rather works to encourage a strong immune system and protection against general injury and illness. It is intended to be a personal spell—i.e., aimed at your own health—but should you wish to promote good health in someone else, keep an image of them at your altar while you work.

<u>You will need:</u>

- A garlic and sage smudge wand
- Light-green candle
- Turquoise, garnet, and clear quartz
- Large fireproof dish

<u>Steps:</u>

Place your crystals on your dish and place the dish in front of your candle. Ignite your candle. Use the flame of the candle to ignite your smudge wand, and then pass the wand over your crystals. As you do this, recite the following:

To fight off pain and disease,

To move through life with ease.

Let the body be happy and healthy.

So mote it be.

Place your smudge stick in the dish next to your crystals and allow it to extinguish naturally.

A Bath for Quick Healing

<u>Intention:</u>

This isn't technically a spell, but rather an act of self-care that makes use of magickal elements and qualities. If you are feeling unwell or have been injured, and want to get better quickly, this procedure will promote a speedy recovery.

<u>You will need:</u>

- A bath
- White or light-green candle
- Rosemary, juniper, and sandalwood essential oils
- Sea salt (3 tbsp)
- Turquoise or a sprig of thyme

<u>Steps:</u>

Light your candle and place the turquoise or thyme next to it. You may also light other candles for atmosphere, as long as one of them is the correct color. Fill your bath around halfway with hot water and sprinkle in the salt. Fill the rest of the bath to your desired temperature and add in the essential oils (one or two drops of each). If you want to include some form of soap or bubble bath, make sure it is unscented.

Relax and enjoy your bath, perhaps playing some music that you find soothing. While you are soaking, visualize a warm light radiating around your area of illness or injury and washing away all the pain and illness. When you exit the bath, do not extinguish your candle until all the water has been drained away.

For Mental Well-Being

Intention:

If you, or someone you know, has been in a bit of a mental health slump recently, this spell will promote healing from that. This will work whether they need to recover from something traumatic, need calming down, or have just been feeling depressed lately. This spell will work to banish negative thought and promote a positive state of mind.

You will need:

- A blue candle
- Incense of your choice
- Sea salt (1 tbsp)
- Stick of charcoal
- Dried rosemary
- A symbol of the person who needs healing
- Turquoise
- A dish or bowl

Steps:

Light your candle and use the flame to ignite your incense. The incense should be something that you find soothing, or if you are directing the spell towards someone else, a scent that reminds you of them.

In your dish or bowl, crush and mix together your seal salt, charcoal, and dried rosemary. You can mix these things together using your wand or, if it is large enough, your turquoise. Place the symbol—an image, piece of hair, or personal item of the person who needs healing—on top of this mixture. Place your turquoise on top of the symbol.

Pass your incense stick over the dish and contents while you visualize the negative energy and thoughts leaving your body (or that of the recipient of the spell). Place the incense stick back in the holder, extinguish your candle, and leave the dish and incense at your altar until it naturally extinguishes.

Chapter 9: Spells for the Home

To Find a New Home

Intention:

Are you moving out of your parents' house for the first time? Perhaps your family is growing, and you need a bigger place? Or maybe you're just ready to move on to a new place and start a new phase in your life. Whatever the reason, this spell will help to direct you towards a new home that is right for you.

You will need:

- An image or description of your dream home
- Gold, silver, or orange candle
- Emerald or jade
- Sweet-orange essential oil
- An orange cloth bag

Steps:

Anoint your candle with the essential oil. Place the symbol of your dream home on your altar. This symbol can be a collection of images that resemble the home you are looking for, a list of written descriptors, or listings of places you plan on viewing. Lay your stone or crystal of choice on top of the symbol. Take a moment to visualize yourself living happily in your new home, then recite the following:

A place where I am home and I am happy,

this I ask is brought to me.

So that I may be protected and secure,

this new home is what I ask for.

So mote it be.

Fold up the images or list and place them, along with your emerald/jade, inside an orange cloth bag. Extinguish your candle. Carry this cloth bag on your person when you attend viewings to bring the energy of the spell along with you.

To Bless a New Home

Intention:

The intention with this ritual is to bless a new space—such as a room or a whole house—and promote the growth of positive energy within the walls. This spell has a few more steps than some of the other ones in this book, but it is worth it to make sure the space you are living in is blessed and free from negative energy.

You will need:

- Fennel and basil
- Peppermint essential oil
- A mixture of charcoal and sea salt
- Sage smudge stick
- Water
- A tea light
- Your chalice
- A heat-resistant dish

<u>Steps:</u>

Begin by placing the tea light on/in your dish, but do not light it yet. Next, place a sprig of fennel, a basil leaf, a dash of peppermint oil, and some black salt onto the tea light to anoint it. Lift your dish and carry it to the entrance of your house (or room). Light the tea light, and recite:

This house shall be good. If not so its past, clear this room and let happiness last.

Place the dish down on a surface within that room and clap twice. Clapping will further get rid of any negative vibrations lingering in the space. Repeat this sequence of chanting and clapping in every room that you wish to bless. When you are done, return to your altar and place the dish down. Do not blow out the tea light, but leave it at the altar to extinguish naturally. As it burns down, you can stare into the flame and visualize negativity burning away alongside it.

Light your smudge stick and return to the entrance. Walk around the house and into every room that you walked into previously, and as the sage burns recite:

By the powers of Fire and Air, I cleanse this space.

Fill your chalice with a mixture of water and salt. Return to the entrance and sprinkle the salt water in each of the corners of your space. As you sprinkle, recite:

By the powers of Earth and Water, I cleanse this space.

Finally, return to your altar and recite:

I thank the elements for blessing this house.

So mote it be.

Dispose of your water in a plant pot, garden, river, or any other outdoor area.

Home Protection Jar

Intention:

If your home is in need of some extra protection from the elements, neighborhood vandals, unwanted guests from the material or spiritual realms, or just in general, this spell jar will help with that. As with the quick healing bath, this is not so much a spell in the traditional sense.

You will need:

- An empty glass jar or bottle (with lid)
- Soil
- Two garlic cloves
- Basil or rosemary
- Sea salt (2 tbsps)
- Vinegar or lemon juice
- Smoky quartz or obsidian
- Optional: sage smudge stick

Steps:

Thoroughly wash your glass jar or bottle with warm water and some mild, unscented soap. Fill it around halfway with soil (ideally from your own garden). If you do not have access to soil, sand from your local beach would also suffice. Pour in two tablespoons of sea salt.

Chop, crush, or dice your garlic cloves. Add the garlic into the jar, along with your basil or rosemary. Drop in a dash of vinegar or a squeeze of lemon juice. Place your smoke quartz or obsidian on top of everything and seal your jar tightly. Place this jar by the main entrance of your home.

If you wish, before sealing the jar you could ignite a sage smudge stick and pass it over the top of everything. Then seal it, and carry your smudge stick with you as you place the jar by the door.

Chapter 10: Spells for Protection

Protect a Pet

Intention:

We all love our little furry babies (or scaly babies, or feathery babies...) and would do anything to keep them safe. This super-simple spell will keep your little ones protected from harm, illness, or wandering off and getting lost.

You will need:

- Sea salt
- Sage smudge stick
- Your pet

Steps:

Use your sea salt to create a circle on the floor or a flat surface, making sure it is big enough for your pet to sit inside comfortably. Light your smudge stick and cleanse the air around your pet. As you do this, recite the following:

With my love and this burning sage

I will keep you safe, in this home and in any place.

With my love and this rhyming charm

I will keep you safe, from danger and from harm.

So mote it be.

Place your smudge stick down on a fireproof dish to extinguish naturally (you may also choose to press it into the dish to extinguish manually). Lift your pet out of the circle and give them a little snuggle to secure the spell and remind them that they are loved.

Anti-Theft Spell

Intention:

Use this spell to protect a place—such as a new home, a safe, or a hotel room—against the threat of theft.

You will need:

- A white candle
- A piece of a chain (such as a broken necklace)
- Holly leaves or essential oil
- Obsidian
- A black cloth bag

Steps:

Place the obsidian, chain, and holly leaves (if using) in front of your candle. If you are using essential oil, anoint your candle and then light it. Close your eyes and visualize the chain wrapping around the space you are aiming to protect from theft. Recite the following:

This chain will work to bind and keep this place safe,

No thief shall enter here and find a thing to take.

So mote it be.

Wrap your items in a black cloth bag and secure them. Extinguish your candle. Place the bag close to an entrance of the place you wish to protect, such as a door or a window.

Protect a Loved One

Intention:

If someone you love is in need of some extra protection, this spell will keep them safe. Perhaps they are headed off on a solo adventure, or they've been feeling ill recently, or they're just a bit clumsy. Whatever they need protection from, this will cover it.

You will need:

- A yellow or pink candle
- Smoky quartz
- A clove of garlic
- Sea salt
- Sage smudge stick
- Something that is symbolic of the loved one (a gift they gave you, a photo of them, something that belongs to them, etc.)

Steps:

Place the smoky quartz, garlic, and symbol on your altar. Light your candle. Sprinkle the sea salt in a circle around your items. Use your candle to ignite your smudge stick and pass it over the items. Place the smudge stick down on a fireproof dish, beside your items, and allow it to extinguish naturally. Extinguish your candle. Once the smudge stick has fully extinguished, you can return the symbol to its rightful place, and you can use the garlic for another spell (or in your dinner).

Conclusion

Well, there you have it: everything you could possibly need to know about working with spells as a Wiccan. Whether you are a brand-new Wiccan looking for guidance, or you've been practicing for a while and just needed some inspiration, we hope that this book has been beneficial to your journey. Please feel free to refer back to any part of this book if you are ever feeling stuck. Wicca is a journey that requires you to never stop learning.

Of course, remember that there is a whole world of materials and inspiration out there for you to use, each with their own purposes. We couldn't cover all of the herbs, plants, spices, minerals, materials, scents, and so on that the world provides us with. The world is bursting with divine energy that can be found in so many different places; you could use something different every day for years and still find something new tomorrow.

On that note, it is important to remember to take care of the world around you. If you are using the natural ingredients provided to you by the divine powers, do not abuse them. Take only what can and should be taken, and dispose of everything responsibly. Be resourceful in your practice as well as your daily life.

And not to sound like a broken record once more, but we do want to remind you that this is a personal journey. If you use the wrong essential oil or substitute smoky quartz for pearl, the world isn't going to end. The most important thing is that your intentions are clear, and they are good. You can practice magick with bad intentions too, but remember the Threefold Law: Everything you put out into the universe will come back to you three times. So, we definitely don't suggest acting on bad intentions.

Finally, if you are looking to experiment even further with Wiccan magick and spells, we have two other books in this series that are available on Amazon. The first book is dedicated to Wicca in general, detailing the history of the Wiccan faith and delving into many of the religion's different aspects. Our final book in the series is dedicated to using candles in Wiccan magick. In that book, we take a detailed look at the different candles that can be used. Inside, we take a deep dive into the spiritual power of fire, provide more information on colorful properties, and offer a selection of spells for you to practice yourself. If you're interested in these other books, simply search my name, 'Sarah Rhodes', on Amazon, and you should find all 3 of the books in this series available in Kindle, Paperback, Hardback, and Audiobook editions.

We wish you luck on your Wiccan journey and look forward to welcoming you back anytime you need us. Blessed be!

References

Alexander, S. (2008). *The Everything Wicca & Witchcraft book: Rituals, Spells and Sacred Objects for Everyday Magick.* Adams Media.

Alexander, S., Macgregor, T., & Singer, M. (2012). *The Only Book of Wiccan Spells You'll Ever Need.* Adams Media.

Amythyst Raine, & Gonzalez, A. (2020). *The Essential Guide to Wicca for Beginners: 52 Spells and Rituals Plus Magical History.* Rockridge Press.

Buckland, R. (1995). *Witchcraft From the Inside: Origins of the Fastest Growing Religious Movement in America.* Llewellyn Publications.

Chamberlain, L. (2020). *Wicca for Beginners: A Guide to Wiccan Beliefs, Rituals, Magic & Witchcraft.* Sterling Ethos.

Cougar, M. (2012). *The Sacred Wheel.* new age & spiritual books.

Dunwich, G. (2021). *Wicca Love Spells.* Kensington Publishing Corporation.

Nice, H. (2019). *Wicca: A Modern Guide to Witchcraft & Magick.* Seal Press.

Sabin, T. (2006). *Wicca for Beginners: Fundamentals of Philosophy & Practice.* Llewellyn Publications.

Van, N., & Vernon, K. (2017). *Practical Magic: A Beginner's Guide to Crystals, Horoscopes, Psychics & Spells.* Running Press.

The Wiccan Rede (or Witches' Rede). (n.d.). Web.mit.edu. https://web.mit.edu/pipa/www/rede.html